Stitching
for Motivation and Positivity

Our thoughts shape our reality, and using positive affirmations helps us reprogram our mind to focus on the good, thereby attracting more positivity and success into our lives.

Sakura Mai

Table of contents

Table of contents

General instructions

Before you start

Cross stitching is a great way to express yourself through art, and it can also be used to surround yourself with beautiful positive quotes! If you are looking for the perfect cross stitch pattern that speaks to your heart, then this book is for you. Here we have compiled 30 of the best cross stitch patterns of motivational and inspirational quotes that will surely inspire you as you create your unique artwork.

Fabric

Counted cross-stitch is worked on even-weave fabrics. These fabrics are manufactured specifically for counted-thread embroidery and are woven with the same number of vertical as horizontal threads per inch. The number of threads per inch determines the size of a finished design.

Aida fabric is fantastic for cross stitch as it is an even-weave, it's also a favorite of beginning stitchers because its weave forms distinctive squares in fabric, which makes placing stitches easily and allows you to create straight lines while you stitch, Aida is measured by "count", 14 count Aida has 14 squares per inch, 18 count has 18 squares per inch = the more squares per inch, the smaller the stitches and overall pattern will be.

Number of strands

The number of strands used varies depending on the fabric. Generally, the rule to follow for cross-stitching is three strands in Aida 11, two strands on Aida 14, one or two strands on Aida 18 (depending on the desired thickness of stitches), and one strand on Hardanger 22. For backstitching, use one strand on all fabrics.

Preparing the fabric

Cut the fabric at least 3 inches larger on each side than the finished design size to ensure enough space for the desired assembly. To prevent fraying, whipstitch, machine-zigzag, or apply a masking tape along the raw edges.

Cleaning the finished design

When you are finished, you can give your fabric a gentle hand wash in cold water and mild soap. Rinse well and roll in a towel to remove excess water. Don't wring, just place it face down on a dry towel and iron on a warm setting until the fabric is dry.

Cross stitch

Danish method

Consist of doing one half of the stitch in one direction, then coming back to do the other half of the stitch, stitches are done in a row or, if necessary, one at a time in an area.
This method is ideal for working in big blocks of color, as you can go in one direction then back ending up at the beginning of the next row or column. This method uses less treads and leaves the back of your work neat.

Steps:
1. Insert needle up between interlacing threads at A.
2. Go down at B. the opening diagonally across from A.
3. Come up at C and go down at D, etc.
4. To complete the top stitches creating an "X" come up at E and go down at B, come up at C and go down at

F, etc. All top stitches should be in the same direction.

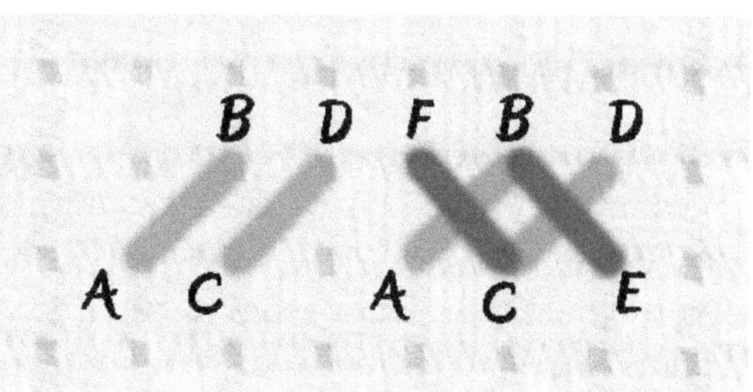

English method

Consist of completing each cross at once, it's often the easier method to use when handling some randomly scattered stitches of one color across your pattern.

Steps:
1. Insert needle up between interlacing threads at A.
2. Go down at B. the opening diagonally across from A.
3. Come up at C and go down at D to complete a full "X".
4. To continue the second "X" come up at E and go down at D, come up at B and go down at F, etc...

There is no right or wrong way to do cross stitch and It's all about experimenting with both methods, the more you stitch, the more you will discover your own rhythm and see which one works best for you most of the time.

Backstitch

Back stitching is usually used for an intricate and detailed design. Though it is not required by the patterns of this book, you can still add it when you feel it's needed.

Steps:
Insert needle up between interlacing threads at A.
Go down at B. one opening to the right.
Come up at C.
Go down at A. one opening to the right.

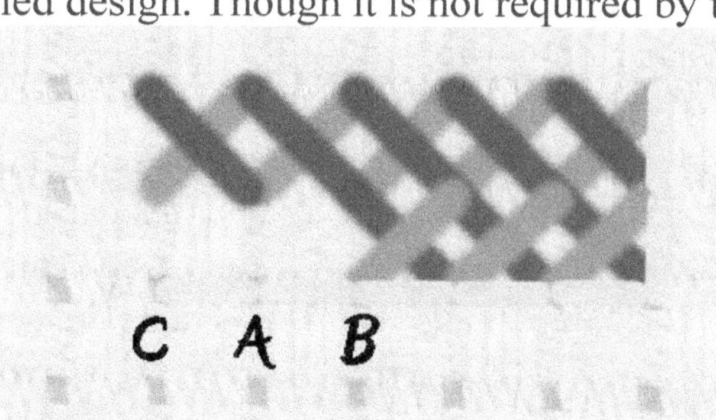

Stitching Blends

This is a new technique for stitching blends where half stitches are done with one color and then half stitches in the opposite direction are done with a second color. By stitching the colors separately, a more even gradient is produced. The choice of lighter or darker color on top affects the middle color, with the lighter color on top producing a lighter middle and the darker color on top producing a darker middle. The general preference is the lighter color on top for a better blend.

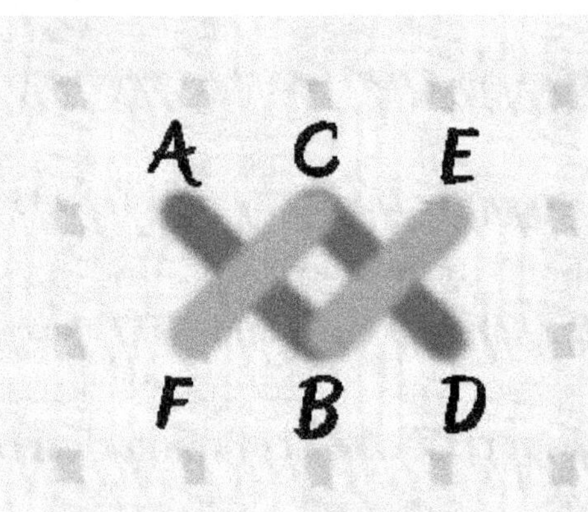

example: DMC-211*   lavender - lt + DMC-3746   blue violet - dk

How to adjust the patterns to be bigger or smaller?

The simplest method is to use the pattern as is, but you need to alter the size or count number of your Aida cloth!
If you would like your design to be larger, use a smaller count, such as 6, 8, or 11 count Aida cloth, which has larger squares (fewer squares per inch) and can make your finished design larger. This method will work if you'd prefer to reduce your pattern size too, just use less count Aida like 18 or 24, and your finished design will come out smaller.

How to figure out how much bigger (or smaller) it will be?

The general rule is simple! Here's the math:
Stitch count of design / Aida cloth count = finished size in inches
Note that you will have to make 2 calculations: 1 for the length and 1 for the width.
Example: We have 28 squares in the width and let's say we decide to use 14 squares of Aida fabric :
28 stitches / 14 count Aida = 2 inch

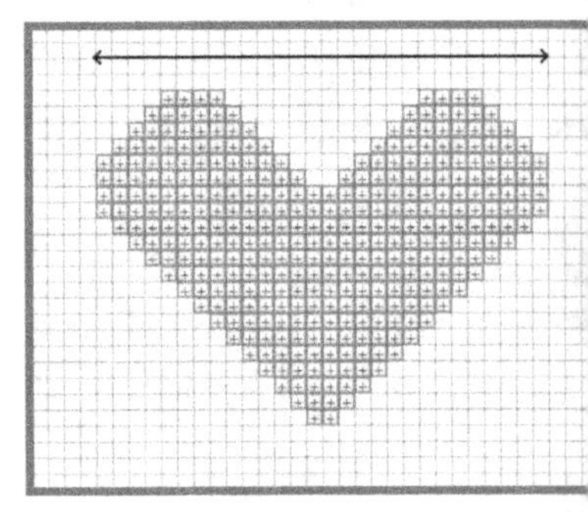

These are approximatively the dimensions rule for all the patterns in this book:
Final fabric dimensions for 7 squares per inch fabric: 25.00x33.29 inches
Final fabric dimensions for 10 squares per inch fabric: 17.50x23.30 inches
Final fabric dimensions for 11 squares per inch fabric: 15.91x21.18 inches
Final fabric dimensions for 12 squares per inch fabric: 14.58x19.42 inches
Final fabric dimensions for 14 squares per inch fabric: 12.50x16.64 inches
Final fabric dimensions for 16 squares per inch fabric: 10.94x14.56 inches
Final fabric dimensions for 18 squares per inch fabric: 9.72x12.94 inches
Final fabric dimensions for 20 squares per inch fabric: 8.75x11.65 inches
Final fabric dimensions for 22 squares per inch fabric: 7.95x10.59 inches
Final fabric dimensions for 24 squares per inch fabric: 7.29x9.71 inches
Final fabric dimensions for 25 squares per inch fabric: 7.00x9.32 inches
Final fabric dimensions for 28 squares per inch fabric: 6.25x8.32 inches
Final fabric dimensions for 58,3 squares per inch fabric: 3.00x4.00 inches

Attitude
IS A LITTLE THING
that makes
A BIG DIFFERENCE

Attitude is a little thing that makes a big difference

Your attitude reflects your mindset, beliefs, and values, which in turn shapes your behavior and actions. By having a positive attitude, you attract positivity into your life. This means that you see opportunities where others see obstacles, and you approach challenges with an open mind. A positive attitude also helps you build strong relationships with people as it radiates warmth and kindness. On the other hand, a negative attitude can bring about negative outcomes. You may feel demotivated or discouraged when faced with difficulties because of pessimistic thinking patterns. Negative attitudes can also drive people away as they may find it difficult to connect with someone who always sees the worst in things.

DMC-519   sky blue
DMC-758   terra cotta - vy lt
DMC-776   pink - md
DMC-967   apricot - vy lt
DMC-3847 teal green - dk
DMC-White white

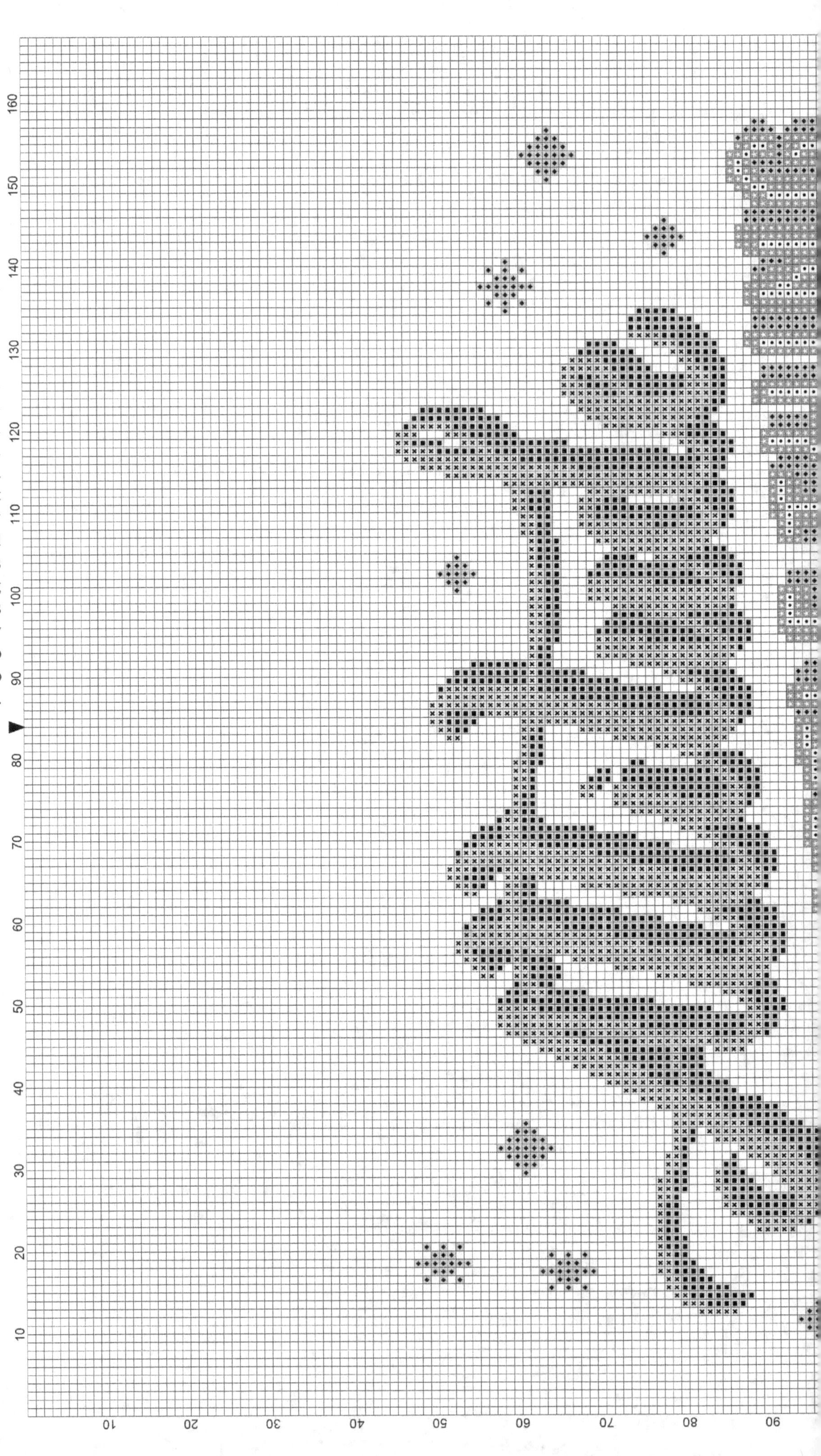

1

LITTLE THINGS
BIG DIFFERENCE

Do you often find yourself in a negative mindset, feeling overwhelmed by life's challenges? It may be time to shift your perspective and embrace the power of positivity. Being positive doesn't mean ignoring or denying the existence of difficulties or problems. Instead, it means approaching those challenges with a can-do attitude and seeking out solutions rather than dwelling on negativity. By choosing positivity, you open yourself up to new opportunities and experiences that may have otherwise been overlooked. Incorporating positivity into your daily routine can bring about numerous benefits such as improved mental health, increased self-esteem, and enhanced relationships with others. So next time you're faced with a hurdle, remember the power of being positive and how it can transform your mindset for the better.

DMC-310   black
DMC-444   lemon - dk
DMC-581   moss green
DMC-608   bright orange
DMC-823   navy blue - dk
DMC-986   forest green - vy dk
DMC-3831   raspberry - dk

You are on a mission to become the best possible version of yourself, and it all starts with your mindset. You should strive to reach your full potential in every aspect of your life. It's not about comparing yourself to others or trying to be someone else; it's about focusing on becoming the best possible version of YOU. To achieve this, you need to take an honest look at yourself and identify areas where you can improve. This may involve setting goals, developing new skills, or simply changing your attitude towards certain things. Remember that becoming the best version of yourself is a journey, not a destination — so don't get discouraged if progress seems slow at times. Ultimately, being the best version of yourself means living up to your own standards and fulfilling your true potential. ▶

DMC-5	driftwood - lt
DMC-900	burnt orange - dk
DMC-992	aquamarine - lt
DMC-3811	turquoise - vy lt

OF YOURSELF.

Believe in yourself

Do you struggle with self-doubt and second-guessing yourself? Have you ever found yourself hesitating to pursue your dreams because of a lack of confidence in your abilities? «Believe in yourself» is a quote that reminds you to have faith in your own capabilities, even when faced with challenges or setbacks. When you believe in yourself, it means that you trust your own judgment and know that you are capable of achieving success. It means having the courage to take risks and pursue your goals, even if they seem daunting at first. Believing in yourself also means being kind to yourself and allowing room for mistakes as part of the learning process. Ultimately, believing in yourself is about recognizing the value and potential within you. It's about understanding that no one else can determine your worth or dictate what you are capable of achieving.

DMC-310   black
DMC-904   parrot green - vy dk
DMC-957   geranium - pl
DMC-3806   cyclamen pink - lt
DMC-3881   avocado green - pl
DMC-White   white

IN
yourself

Bravo

Bravo is a word that signifies praise and congratulations. Saying «bravo» to yourself can have an empowering effect on your mindset. When you achieve something great, it's important to take a moment to acknowledge it and give yourself credit for your hard work. Saying «bravo» to yourself can help you celebrate your own achievements and build up self-confidence. By recognizing your own successes, you are less likely to fall into negative self-talk patterns and more likely to continue striving towards your goals. In addition, saying «bravo» can also create a positive energy around you that inspires others as well. When we see someone else succeed, it can motivate us to push ourselves further towards our own goals.

DMC-722   orange spice - lt
DMC-743   yellow - md
DMC-798   delft blue - dk
DMC-800   delft blue - pl
DMC-921   copper
DMC-3810 turquoise - dk

Collect adventures not things

Rather than spending your money on things that will eventually lose their value or become outdated, invest in creating memories that will last a lifetime. When you collect adventures, you're opening yourself up to new perspectives, cultures, and ways of life. It's about putting yourself out there and stepping out of your comfort zone. Whether it's trying exotic food or taking part in adrenaline-pumping activities like skydiving or bungee jumping, these are the moments that truly make life worth living. In essence, this quote is a reminder to live fully and not get bogged down by the trappings of consumerism.

DMC-26   lavender - pale
DMC-31   blueberry
DMC-3824 apricot - lt
DMC-3887 lavender - ul vy dk

ADVENTURES
things

Have you ever felt like life is just a series of grey, gloomy days? Days where the sun doesn't shine and everything seems to be going wrong? It's easy to get stuck in this mindset, but there's a quote that can help shake you out of it: «Create your own sunshine.» This simple phrase means that you have the power to make your own happiness and positivity. You don't have to wait for external factors to bring joy into your life; instead, you can cultivate it within yourself. When you create your own sunshine, you become the master of your emotions. You realize that happiness is not something that happens to you - it's something that comes from within. By taking control of your attitude and outlook on life, you can brighten even the darkest day.

DMC-341	blue violet - lt	
DMC-351	coral	
DMC-352	coral -lt	
DMC-725	topaz	
DMC-741	tangerine - md	
DMC-938	coffee brown - ul dk	
DMC-3345	hunter green - dk	
DMC-3347	yellow green - md	
DMC-3363	pine green - md	
DMC-3863	mocha beige - md	
DMC-White	white	

When you dance with fairies, you're tapping into a magical realm where anything is possible. You're letting go of inhibitions and surrendering to the moment. Riding a unicorn may seem like a far-fetched fantasy, but it's symbolic of chasing your dreams and believing in the impossible. Swimming with mermaids represents exploring the unknown depths of yourself and the world around you. And chasing rainbows? That's all about finding beauty in unexpected places. So take this quote as an invitation to step outside your comfort zone and follow your heart wherever it takes you.

DMC-211* lavender - lt + DMC-3746 blue violet - dk
DMC-211 lavender - lt
DMC-307 lemon
DMC-310 black
DMC-606 burnt orange-red
DMC-740 tangerine
DMC-958 seagreen - dk
DMC-3608 plum - vy lt
DMC-3746 blue violet - dk
DMC-3843* electric blue + DMC-958 seagreen - dk
DMC-3891 turquoise - vy dk br

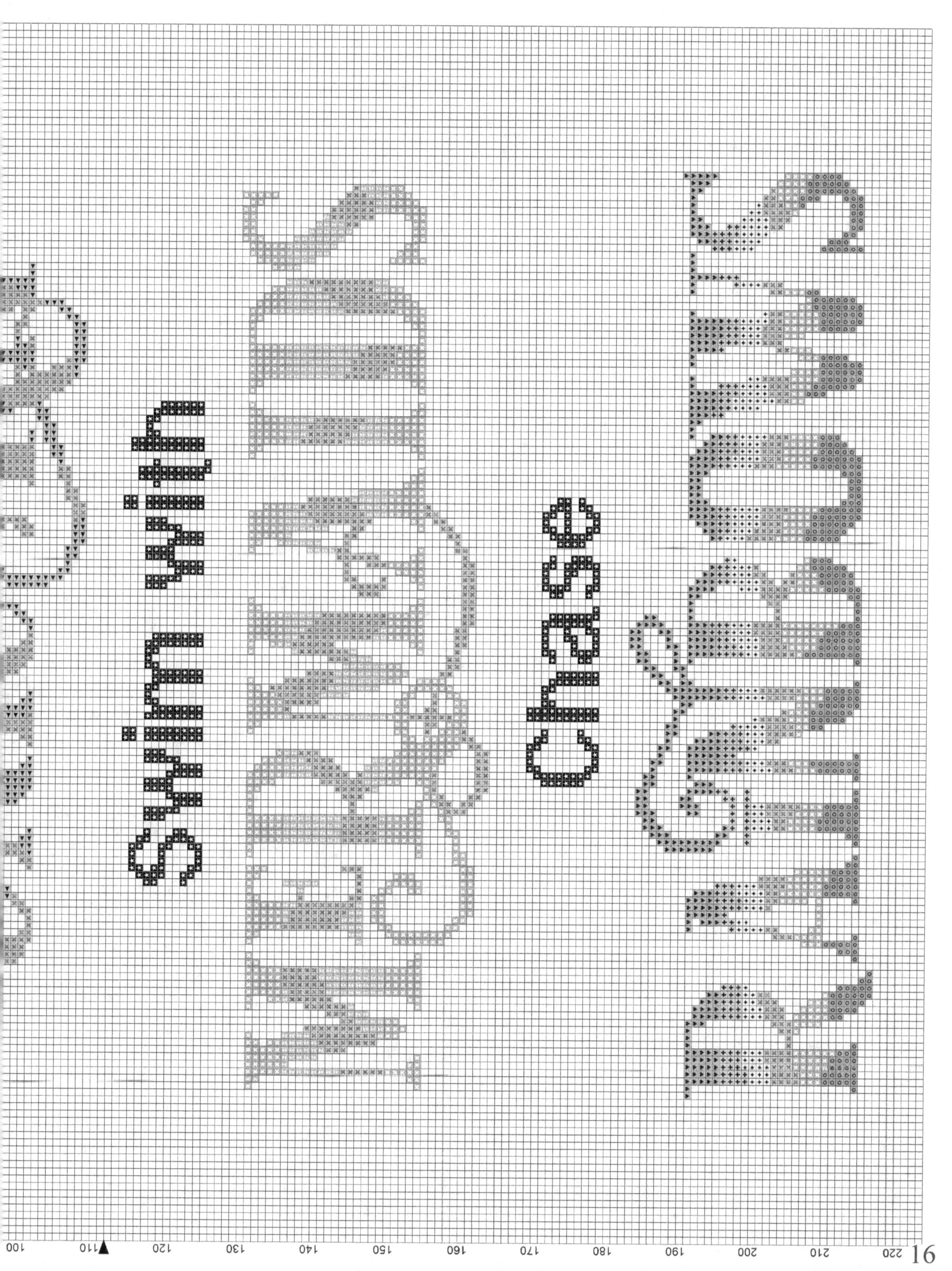

Do your best

Do you often wonder what it means to «do your best»? It's a common phrase that many people hear from parents, teachers or coaches, but sometimes it can be hard to understand what it truly entails. Essentially, doing your best means putting forth the maximum amount of effort and energy into something, whether it be a task or goal. It's about giving it your all and not holding back. When you strive to do your best, you're setting yourself up for success. You're giving yourself the opportunity to showcase your talents and abilities in their truest form. Doing your best ensures that you're putting in 100% effort into everything that you do without any shortcuts or half-hearted attempts. By doing so, you increase the likelihood of achieving bigger and better things than if you were just coasting by.

DMC-336 navy blue
DMC-813 blue - lt

Focus on the good

Do you ever find yourself feeling overwhelmed by the negative things in your life? It's easy to get caught up in all of the stress and challenges that come our way, but it's important to remember that there is always good to be found. The quote «focus on the good» is a powerful reminder to shift our perspective and look for positivity in every situation. When you choose to focus on the good, you are choosing to see the world through a lens of gratitude and appreciation. Instead of dwelling on what went wrong or what could have been better, you are actively looking for the silver lining. This mindset can have a profound impact on your overall outlook on life and your mental health. Furthermore, focusing on the good can also improve your relationships with others. When we approach interactions with a positive attitude, we are more likely to attract positive energy from those around us.

DMC-892   carnation - md
DMC-939   navy blue - vy dk
DMC-958   seagreen - dk
DMC-3811 turquoise - vy lt

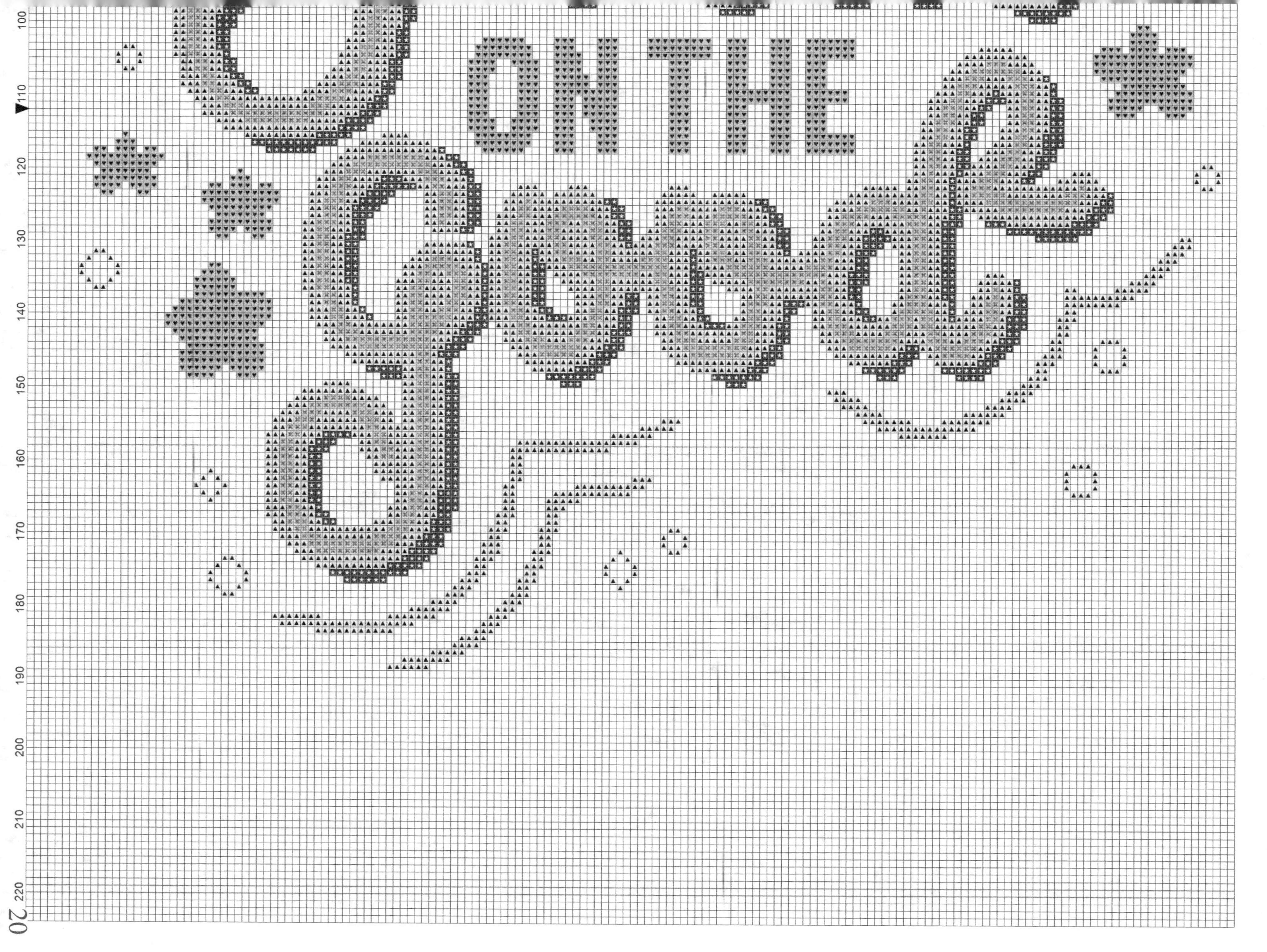
ON THE
good

BELIEVE
IN
yourself

Collect
ADVENTURES
not
things

Go where you feel most alive

You wake up in the morning, feeling groggy and uninspired. Your day is planned out with a long list of appointments and errands that you dread doing. You think you are trapped in a routine, completing the same tasks day after day. But then, as you sip your coffee and take a deep breath, you remember those words: «Go where you feel most alive.» Suddenly, your mind starts to race with possibilities. You think about all the places that make you feel truly happy - whether it's hiking up a mountain trail or strolling along the beach at sunset. The idea of breaking free from your routine and experiencing something new fills you with excitement and energy. As the day goes on, you keep that quote close to your heart.

DMC-597 turquoise
DMC-3340 apricot - md
DMC-3814 spring marine
DMC-3886 mocha brown - lu av tf

No matter your age or circumstances, you can always begin again. Whether it's learning a new skill, starting a new career path, or even pursuing a long-held dream, there is no expiration date on the opportunities available to you. Perhaps you've been hesitant to take the leap and try something new because of fear of failure or uncertainty about what lies ahead. However, this quote encourages you to embrace those feelings as part of the journey towards growth and progress. Even if your first attempts don't go as planned, every step forward brings valuable lessons and experiences that will ultimately lead you closer to your goals. Remember that life is full of twists and turns, and sometimes unexpected events lead us down paths we never imagined for ourselves. do not define your future. It's a way to motivate yourself to take a step forward and to not let fear or self-doubt hold you back.

DMC-741   tangerine - md + DMC-742   tangerine - lt
DMC-741*   tangerine - md
DMC-742   tangerine - lt
DMC-798   delft blue - dk
DMC-823   navy blue - dk
DMC-915   plum - dk
DMC-3806   cyclamen pink - lt
DMC-3890   turquoise - vy lt br
DMC-White white

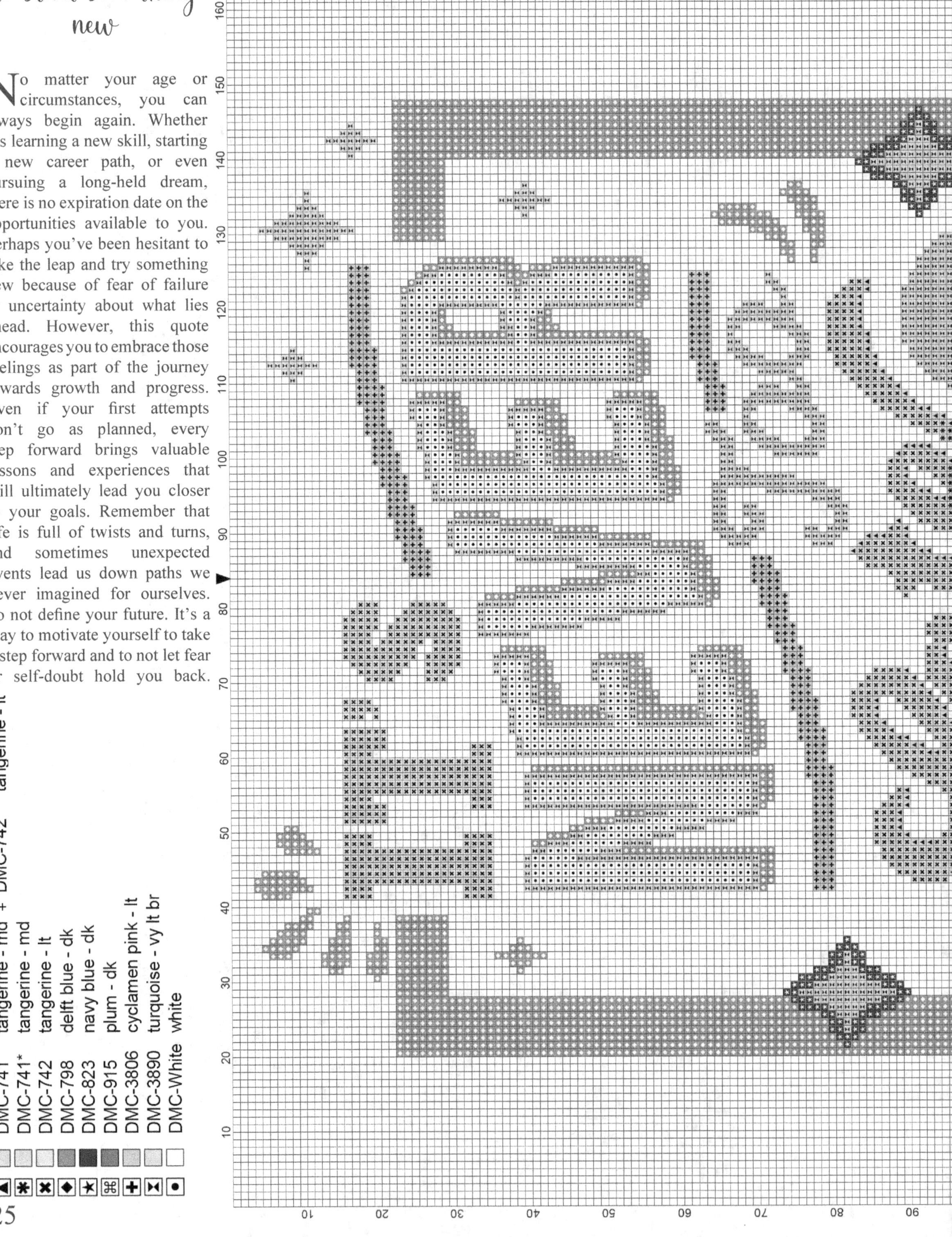

25

START
SOMETHING
NEW

It's time to believe in you

You've been telling yourself that you're not good enough for far too long. It's time to change that mindset and start believing in yourself. This quote is a powerful reminder that you have the ability to achieve great things if only you would have faith in yourself. You may have experienced setbacks or failures in the past, but they don't define who you are as a person. Look at them as opportunities to learn and grow instead of reasons to doubt your abilities. Believe in your strengths, talents, and unique qualities – these are what make you special. When self-doubt creeps up, remind yourself of all the times when you did succeed or overcame challenges. Celebrate those victories and use them as fuel to keep going forward towards your goals.

DMC-307 lemon
DMC-907 parrot green - lt
DMC-3607 plum - lt
DMC-3837 lavender - ul dk
DMC-3846 bright turquoise - lt

Are you just going through the motions day by day, and nothing ever seems to ever change? Does it seem like your current path is leading you up the same dead-end road? Right now, it's a good time to step outside your comfort zone. It means that real growth and progress can only happen when you step outside of what's familiar and safe. When you challenge yourself to try new things, take risks, and embrace uncertainty, that's when you truly start living. And while it might be scary at first, pushing yourself beyond your limits can lead to incredible personal growth. So don't be afraid to break the routine and try something new.

DMC-310 black
DMC-444 lemon - dk
DMC-992 aquamarine - lt
DMC-3847 teal green - dk

· OF YOUR
Comfort
Zone

Life is journey
Enjoy the ride

You wake up and begin your day. You have a plan, a goal, something that you want to achieve. But what about the journey? Do you take time to enjoy it or are you solely focused on the end result? This quote reminds you that each step of your life is valuable and deserves to be cherished. Think about your fondest memories. Was it just reaching your destination or was it also the moments leading up to it? Life is full of unexpected surprises and obstacles, but these moments often shape us into who we are today. By embracing each twist and turn in our path, we learn more about ourselves and gain appreciation for what we have. The ride may not always be easy or smooth sailing, but it's important to remember that every experience contributes to our personal growth.

DMC-307   lemon
DMC-803   baby blue - ul vy dk
DMC-3846 bright turquoise - lt

The Ride

To understand this quote better, you need to think about the purpose of a compass and a clock. A compass shows you the direction while a clock shows you time. Living your life like a compass means that you are more focused on finding your own path in life rather than obsessing over time. Time is something that we can never get back, but if we use our time wisely and set our goals based on what truly matters to us, then we will be able to create a fulfilling life for ourselves. Just like how a compass helps guide us in the right direction when we're lost or unsure of where to go next.

DMC-310	black
DMC-967	apricot - vy lt
DMC-3340	apricot - md
DMC-3340*	apricot - md + DMC-3705 melon - dk
DMC-3705	melon - dk
DMC-White	white

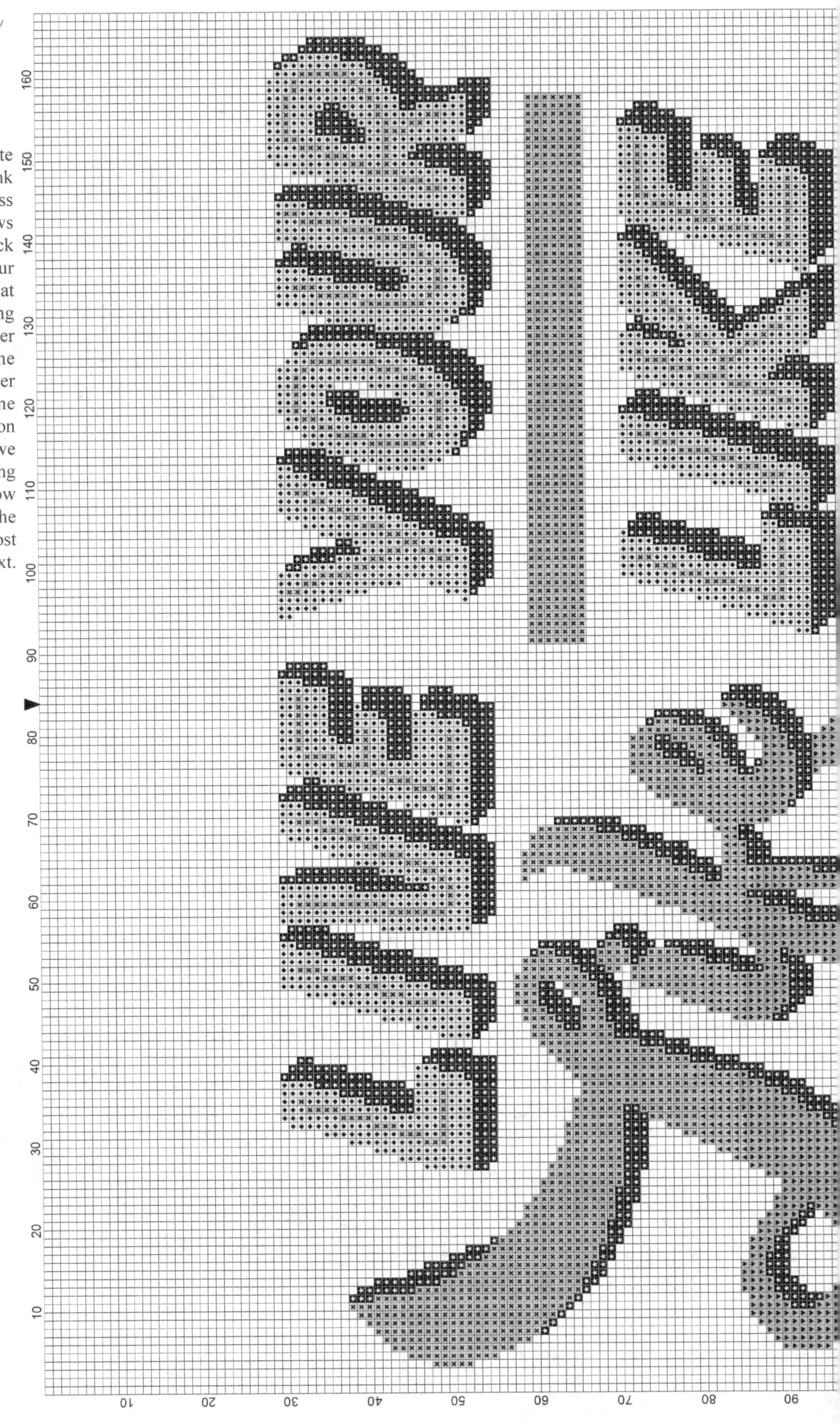

COMPASS
NOT A Clock

Love yourself

Love yourself, two simple words with a profound meaning. It is about accepting who you are and treating yourself with kindness, respect, and compassion. You need to love yourself for who you are before you can start to truly love others. The journey of self-love requires patience, self-awareness, and positivity. It begins by acknowledging your strengths instead of focusing on your weaknesses. Recognize that nobody is perfect and that it's okay to make mistakes. Learn from them and grow as an individual. Treat yourself like you would treat your best friend - be supportive, encouraging, and understanding. Self-love also means setting boundaries for yourself and learning to say no when necessary. Don't let others take advantage of you or manipulate you into doing something against your will. It's important to prioritize your needs before fulfilling the needs of others.

Make your dreams happen

You have the power to turn your dreams into reality. You are capable of achieving anything you set your mind to, as long as you put in the effort and take action towards making those dreams a reality. When you make your dreams happen, it's not just about achieving success or reaching a certain goal. It's about living a life that is fulfilling and meaningful to you. It's about pursuing what truly makes you happy and bringing those aspirations to life. So how do you make your dreams happen? First, identify what those dreams are - whether it's starting a business, traveling the world, or learning a new skill - and then start taking actionable steps towards making them happen.

DMC-310   black
DMC-727* topaz - vy lt + DMC-973   canary - br
DMC-973   canary - br
DMC-3809 turquoise - vy dk

37

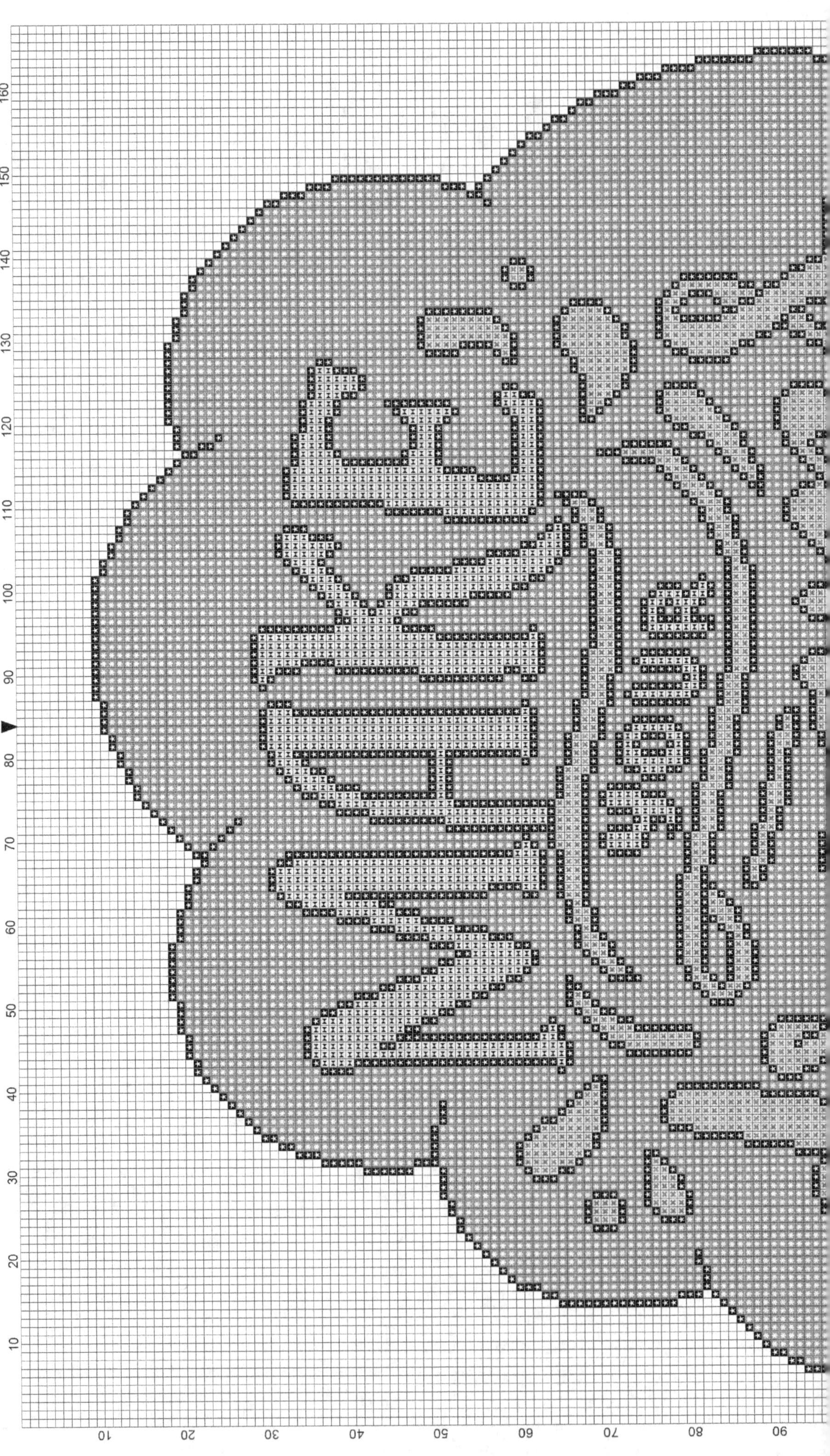

HAPPEN

Make yourself a priority

You are important, and it's time to start treating yourself like you are. You spend so much time focusing on other people's needs and wants that you often forget to take care of yourself. But making yourself a priority is essential if you want to live a happy, healthy life. When you make yourself a priority, you give yourself permission to say «no» when something doesn't serve your best interests. You prioritize your health by eating well and getting enough sleep. You take the time to exercise regularly because you know how good it makes you feel both physically and mentally. Making yourself a priority doesn't mean being selfish or neglecting others - it means recognizing that in order to be the best version of yourself for others, you need to first take care of your own needs.

DMC-501
DMC-742
DMC-948
DMC-White

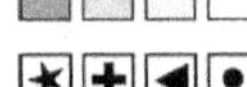

100 110 120 130 140 150 160 170 180 190 200 210 220
40

Rainbow in someone else's cloud

The idea behind this quote is that we all have the power to brighten someone else's day. By being a source of positivity and encouragement for others, we not only help them through their struggles but also uplift ourselves in the process. Whether it's offering a kind word or gesture, lending an ear to listen or simply being a shoulder to lean on, there are countless ways we can bring joy into someone else's life.

DMC-19	autumn gold - md lt
DMC-310	black
DMC-729	old gold - md
DMC-917	plum - md
DMC-961	dusty rose - dk
DMC-991	aquamarine - dk
DMC-3325	baby blue - lt
DMC-3809	turquoise - vy dk
DMC-3851	bright green - lt
DMC-White	white

Someone
else's
CLOUD

MAKE,
YOUR
dreams
HAPPEN

Strive
for
Progress
not
perfection

When you strive for perfection, it can be easy to become discouraged and give up when things don't go exactly as planned. However, if you focus on making progress instead, you will be able to see the small steps forward that you are making towards your ultimate goal. This approach can help keep you motivated and moving forward. The key takeaway from this quote is to not get bogged down by striving for an unattainable level of perfection. Instead, celebrate each step forward in achieving your goals and continue working hard towards them.

DMC-601 cranberry - dk
DMC-604 cranberry - lt
DMC-3842 wedgewood - vy dk
DMC-3844* bright turquoise - dk

Progress not perfection

Take time to make your soul happy

You wake up every morning with a long list of tasks to accomplish. You work hard all day, ticking off items on your to-do list one by one. But do you ever stop and think about what truly makes you happy? In the midst of this busy routine, it's easy to forget that our souls need nourishment too. When we neglect our inner selves, it can lead to feelings of emptiness and dissatisfaction, even when things on the surface seem fine. Taking time for self-care activities like reading a book, practicing yoga or meditation or simply spending time in nature can help recharge your batteries and remind you of what really matters in life. their progress along the way. By doing so, people can maintain a positive outlook, stay motivated, and keep moving forward towards their desired outcomes.

DMC-1 — white tin
DMC-336 — navy blue
DMC-721 — orange spice - md
DMC-943 — aquamarine - md
DMC-964 — seagreen - lt
DMC-3341 — apricot
DMC-3818 — emerald green - ul vy dk

The best way to predict the future is to create it

Instead of waiting for things to happen, you should take action and make things happen yourself. By doing so, you not only have control over your own future but also influence the direction in which society as a whole is headed. If you want to achieve success in any area of your life, whether it's personal or professional, creating your own path is key. You cannot sit around waiting for opportunities to come knocking at your door. Instead, you need to actively seek out opportunities and put in the hard work required to make them a reality. This isn't an activity for the faint of heart; it takes risk and requires stepping out of your comfort zone. When you create your own future, there's no limit on what you can achieve. we choose the right steps and act accordingly. It encourages us to think about how we can make positive changes in order for our lives, families, careers and communities to move forward in meaningful ways.

DMC-1   white tin
DMC-311   navy blue - md
DMC-3890   turquoise - vy lt br

THE FUTURE
is
create it

When it comes to loving yourself, it's not just about feeling good in your own skin. Loving yourself means taking care of your emotional well-being and setting boundaries for what you will and won't tolerate from others. This quote is a reminder that when we prioritize our own self-love, we are less likely to put up with people or situations that don't serve us. We become more discerning about who we allow into our lives and how they treat us. This doesn't mean being selfish or closed off; rather, it means valuing ourselves enough to say no to things that don't align with our values. As you learn to love yourself more fully, you may find that some relationships or habits fall away naturally. You might also discover new opportunities and connections that support your growth and happiness.

DMC-727 topaz - vy lt
DMC-892 carnation - md
DMC-3746 blue violet - dk
DMC-3812 sea green - vy dk
DMC-3892 orange spice - md lt

You've been feeling defeated lately, like you want to give up on your dreams or goals. It's easy to get caught up in the negative thoughts and let them consume you. But have you stopped to think about why you started in the first place? What inspired you to pursue your passion? When you feel like quitting, take a moment to reflect on that initial spark of inspiration. Remember the excitement and energy that propelled you forward towards your goal. Think about all the hard work and dedication you've put into it so far, and how much progress you've made. It's okay to feel discouraged at times, but don't let those feelings overshadow all of your accomplishments thus far. Keep pushing forward with determination and focus. When doubt creeps in, remind yourself of why you started and use that as motivation to keep going.

DMC-11	tender green - lt
DMC-959	seagreen - md
DMC-3608	plum - vy lt
DMC-3823	yellow - ul pl
DMC-White	white

55

THINK ABOUT
why you

When you embark on any journey or pursue any goal, it's crucial to pour all of your passion and energy into it. This quote reminds us that half-hearted efforts will only lead to mediocrity. As you set out on your own path in life, keep this quote close to your heart. Whether you're starting a new job, pursuing a new hobby or traveling to a new destination, approach it with enthusiasm and an unwavering commitment. Don't hold back - throw yourself into every task with everything you've got! When things get tough (and they inevitably will), remember that giving up is not an option.

DMC-351   coral
DMC-597   turquoise
DMC-598   turquoise - lt
DMC-3705 melon - dk
DMC-3706 melon - md
DMC-3808 turquoise - ul vy dk
DMC-Ecru ecru

Your heart

You are beautiful

You are the embodiment of beauty. Every curve, every freckle, every imperfection is a unique and perfect piece of you. Your radiance does not come from your physical appearance alone, but from the way you carry yourself with grace and confidence. You are so much more than just a pretty face; your mind is sharp, your heart is kind, and your spirit is unstoppable. It's easy to get caught up in our own insecurities and doubts about our self-worth. But it's important to remember that we all have value simply by existing. You are no exception to this rule - in fact, you shine brighter than most! Your inner beauty shines through in everything you do: how you treat others with kindness and compassion, how you pursue your passions with determination and joy. So don't let anyone, not even yourself, convince you otherwise

DMC-310   black
DMC-501   blue green - dk
DMC-741   tangerine - md
DMC-972   canary - dp
DMC-3347   yellow green - md
DMC-3771   terra cotta - ul vy lt
DMC-3804   cyclamen pink - dk
DMC-3806   cyclamen pink - lt
DMC-White white

You are capable of amazing things

You are capable of amazing things. Don't let anyone or anything tell you otherwise. The potential lies within you; it's up to you to tap into it and unleash the greatness that awaits. Believe in yourself, even when others doubt your abilities. Remember that success is not defined by external factors, but rather by your own personal growth and achievements. Embrace challenges as opportunities for growth and learning, and don't be afraid to take risks. In a world where negativity can sometimes feel overwhelming, remember that your mindset is key. Believe in your own strength and capability to overcome obstacles and achieve greatness. You have the power within you to make a difference - so go out there and show the world what you're made of!

DMC-35   fuschia - vy dk
DMC-606   burnt orange-red
DMC-3761   sky blue - lt
DMC-3845   bright turquoise - md
DMC-White   white

You are in control of your own destiny, and everything in your life is completely up to you. You have the power to create the life that you want for yourself, and it is up to you to make it happen. When you think about this quote, it can be empowering because it means that you have complete control over your own happiness and success. You don't have to rely on anyone else to make things happen for you, because everything comes from within. You can choose how much effort you put into achieving your goals, and how much time and energy you dedicate towards them. No matter what obstacles come your way, remember that you are the artist of your own life. You have the ability to overcome any challenge or adversity if you truly believe in yourself and stay committed to reaching your goals. ▶

DMC-500	blue green - vy dk	
DMC-964	seagreen - lt	
DMC-3844	bright turquoise - dk	
DMC-3845	bright turquoise - md	
DMC-White	white